This Book Belongs To:
____

BY
Home Planners And
Journals
To help you organize your life

This book is copyright protected. Reproducing this book is prohibited and not allowed without the permission of the author. All rights reserved.

www.ingramcontent.com/pod-product-compliance
Lightning Source LLC
Chambersburg PA
CBHW071221240726
48654CB00009B/879